The Punkawallah's Rope

Chrys Salt

Indigo Dreams Publishing

First Edition: The Punkawallah's Rope
First published in Great Britain in 2017 by:
Indigo Dreams Publishing
24, Forest Houses
Cookworthy Moor
Halwill
Beaworthy
Devon
EX21 5UU
www.indigodreams.co.uk

Chrys Salt has asserted her right under the Copyright, Designs and Patents Act 1988 to be identified as the author of this work.
© Chrys Salt 2017

ISBN 978-1-910834-59-6

British Library Cataloguing in Publication Data. A CIP record for this book can be obtained from the British Library.

This book is sold subject to the condition that it shall not, by way of trade or otherwise, be lent, re-sold, hired out, or otherwise circulated without the author's and publisher's prior consent in any form of binding or cover other than that in which it is published and without a similar condition including this condition being imposed on the subsequent purchaser.

Designed and typeset in Palatino Linotype by Indigo Dreams.
Author cartoon illustration by Alban Low.
Cover design by Ronnie Goodyer of Indigo Dreams.
Printed and bound in Great Britain by 4edge Ltd.
www.4edge.co.uk.

Papers used by Indigo Dreams are recyclable products made from wood grown in sustainable forests following the guidance of the Forest Stewardship Council.

*For Professor Bimalendu Bhattacharya
from his 'only English daughter'
and Professor Bashabi Fraser and Neil Fraser
for their friendship and for introducing me to India.*

Acknowledgements

Many thanks to my friends Elspeth Brown and Donald Adamson for their patient advice and suggestions, my husband Richard, who keeps my spirits from the doldrums of self-doubt and Ronnie and Dawn at Indigo Dreams who give my work such a loving and supportive home.

Poems from *The Punkawallah's Rope* have appeared in Southlight Issue 21, The Café Review and Thali Katori: an anthology of Scottish South Asian Poetry and The Glasgow Herald.

www.chryssalt.com   for more information on Chrys' books, plays, performance credits and awards.

CONTENTS

Mother India 5
Raju says … 6
Durga's Temple 7
Raju says … 8
Hanuman's Temple 8
Raju's advice 9
Dawn journey 10
Sales pitch 10
The Manikarnika Ghat 11
Moksha 14
Sales pitch 15
Raju says … 16
Compassion Goddess 17
Raju says … 18
Saraswati 19
Raju says… 21
The language of the horn 22
Grand Hotel, Kolkata 23
Letter from the Raj (extract 1) 24
Punkawallah 24
Letter from the Raj (extract 2) 26
Partition 1947 26
Flight (The Himalayas 1959) 28
Refuge (Darjeeling 2016) 30
The Scottish Cemetery, Kolkata 32
Departure 34
Dancing girl 34

Mother India

From up here, inlets glitter
bright as knives,
slice slits into the skirts of India.

Inland, a blouse of hills
glows with embroidery
of shadow, amber sun

moulding the breasts
and shoulders of this
gracious continent.

Sand, gold and silken,
frilled with lace, edges the kirtle
of a cornflower sea.

From up here India
is courtly, innocent,
and quite 'The Lady',

not waving amputated stumps
or banging in car windows
with a borrowed baby.

Raju says ...

It is full morning,
and Raju kips on the hard seat
of his rickshaw at our hotel gate,
uncurls as we approach,
yawns, stretches toothpick legs,
applies a grin.
'Today I take you temple.
Durga is woman God,
she kill tigers.
Man look after shoes. You pay him.
No photographs.
Man look after camera.
You pay him.
'No shoes in holy places',
Raju says.

Note: not everything Raju says is accurate! Durga is the Hindu Goddess of power, strength and protection. The tiger (or sometimes a lion) is Durga's steed. Durga does not kill tigers.

Durga's Temple

Barefoot, we slop through water,
fallen flowers and spit.
Durga, not made by man they say,
but here of her own making,
holds court, fierce eyed and garlanded.
Her warrior tiger crouches at her feet.

Gibbering monkeys scratch their bums,
trapeze on chains of holy bells.
No haunting organ, hushed magnificence,
but rackets of rowdy reverence,
amplified chants and mantras,
clangour of gongs and bells.

Beneath the rouged and pillared canopies,
on steps, the floor, on shelves, in crevices,
are offerings of sweets, ghee, plates of fruit,
dishes of cardamom, cloves, betel nut.
Candles stir in terracotta dishes.
Pomegranate mouths gape ruby teeth.

Outside a silver wedding car sits patiently.
Suited and sari'ed devotees
queue on the pavement to leave shoes.
A black kite hovers hungrily
over a blanket laid with fish.

Everyone waits here for something good.

Raju says ...

'I take you clean toilet.
You go piss or stool?'
'Piss,' I say without embarrassment.
'Very clean toilet. 5 rupee.
You pay me what you want.
I take you there.
Has proper pan.
Raju is not a greedy man.'

Hanuman's Temple
'Do not feed monkeys. Creates management problem.'

Nit-picking hairy fingers poke tourists' nibbles
between yellow teeth, threadbare bum
on the gravel. It is a brief eyeballing,
but offence is taken. His wizened little face
gapes to a pink Munch scream.
Eyes round and black with feral spite,
he drops his treat, jabbers with fury,
launches at my jeans,
nips through the denim, misses flesh,
then agile as a tumbler vaults
into the trees. We retreat, leave
the temple to its fractious guardians,
shaken by something primitive, familiar.

Raju's advice

A ragged token of a man
keeps pace with us.
Cups a calloused hand.
'Baksheesh, Baksheesh'.
Our rickshaw gathers speed.
We heed advice
that gifts to one,
invite an avalanche of need.
Breathless the beggar slows,
sneezes an insult of complaint.
A slug of snot
slides slowly down the paint.

Dawn journey

How can I write you,
asleep in the dust,
thin under bundled blankets
on the pavements of Varanasi,
hunkered against shop fronts,
corrugated shutters,
in fruit rotting from yesterday's market,
end to end with another, and another, and another?

How can I write you
without pity making a nuisance of itself,
the poem closing its fist?

We judder down darkened streets,
high on our regal rickshaw,
float prayer candles
on your sacred river,
watch dawn sun
skim gold across the water,
talk to our boatman Bollo
of impossible hopes for his children.

Sales pitch

A small girl on the Ghats,
no more than eight,
eyes dark as pansies,

hair a clotted mess,
shuffles a pack of post cards
like a conjuring trick,
and then in perfect English,
'Why do tourists say no to me?
Why don't tourists say yes?'

The Manikarnika Ghat

A man who calls himself a priest,
invites us in, brooks no dissent.
Our Tourist Guide had warned of this,

and yet, voyeurs to griefs not ours,
we follow him up hollowed steps.
The Ganges bobs with orange flowers.

Candles and faeces swill round boats
of tourists – keen, like us, to see
the sunrise on The Ganges. Goats

tiptoe and bleat round bonfires, swarms
of seabirds swoop above the smoke,
dive-bomb for fish, shriek loud alarms.

The stench of burning hair and bone
assails our nostrils, seeps into the skin,
clings to us like a foul cologne,

with other sweet and sickly scents
of roasting flesh, joss sticks, cow dung,
flaming sandalwood, ghee, incense.

A man in white, his head shaved bare,
chief mourner to one lately dead,
offers a less than kindly glare.

We pick our way past burning pyres,
a dog asleep in human ash.
Mourners play cards amongst the fires.

Another man, half naked, flicks
a charred hand, back into the blaze,
prods it in deeper with a stick,

smashes the head. Our 'priest' explains,
that only when the head explodes,
can souls be free, rise from the flames,

find moksha in this holy place,
escape the cycle of rebirth
and death, makes a compelling case

for charity, a salesman's pitch,
to touch our western consciences.
How 'unburned bodies never reach

moksha', that 'without cremation,
the poor have water burials,
corpses wash up like carrion

on muddy banks for hungry dogs'.
How 'there can be no salvation'
for those who can't afford the logs

of sacred teak and sandalwood,
that 'on the ghats the rich burn bright,
the poor are fish and vulture food'.

He tugs the heartstrings of our purse,
with practised fingers, and although
he smiles, his eyes are dangerous.

We offer cash 'for karma', flee
past funeral pyres, abandoned shrouds,
the chants, the alien obsequies,

the drying corpses, dogs and cows,
head to The Dolphin for our lunch,
wishing we'd bought those postcards now.

Note: in Hinduism and Jainism moksha means release from the cycle of rebirth impelled by the law of karma. The Ghats in Varanasi are riverfront steps leading down to The Ganges. There are 87 of them. A few are used as sacred cremation sites. The man tending the fire would be a Dom, a sub caste of The Untouchables. Only they are allowed to touch dead bodies. Death is thought to be contagious.

Moksha

I'm dressed in saffron
cold on this bamboo.
They carry me down
ancient lanes,
past pans of sizzling paneer,
charcoal fires,
to purify my body
by The Ghats.
What was my life?
A little quest
for nothing much.
I married young, no choice,
he wasn't kind,
miscarried twice and bled,
delivered in the dust
a girl who's coming
split me half in two.
And so I died.
Now in my end do I begin.
Your guilty gift
is my release.
The fire will touch my body
like a kiss.

Sales pitch

Brown and wrinkled as a date,
one breast, deliberately exposed, bare feet,
she prowls the chattering market,
selling the only fruit she has to offer,
so her children can eat.

Raju says ...

We're drinking coffee in a smart cafe.
Raju is wily, quite at home.
'I bring you nice place,' he says,
and asks for chips.
He fishes out a book of testimonials,
in Russian, German, Urdu, Thai.
'I give good service.
People write recommendation.
You speak French? You translate me'.
'Raju meilleur homme de pousse-pousse.'
Raju pokes the page.
'Write me good in English,
Raju best rickshaw man,
you write me, yes?'

Compassion Goddess

How many ears
to hear the sound of sorrow?

How many eyes
to see all ways at once?

How many mouths
to shout into tomorrow?

How many arms
to shield these little ones?

Compassion's not the stuff
of prayer or mantra.

It is not fashioned
out of clay or stone.

It is ourselves
reflected in a mirror,

the god inside ourselves
come home.

Note: in one Buddhist legend Guan Yin (goddess of compassion) is depicted with a thousand arms and a varying numbers of eyes, hands and heads, sometimes with an eye in the palm of each hand, enabling her to see and reach out to anyone in need.

Raju says ...

Raja says he is 50,
has seven children,
three grandchildren.
'I am stupid,' Raju says.
'I take you good place.
I give good service.
I say good history.
You pay me what you want.
Maybe you buy my rickshaw,
now you see my life?'

Note: *many bicycle rickshaw drivers earn less than 100 rupees a day (just over £1.00) and since they can't afford to buy one, they have to hire one, an expense that can eat up 50% of their earnings.*

Saraswati
'She who lives on the tongues of poets'

You were surrounded by fans at your puja.
I couldn't get near you for a chat,
and I wanted to ask for something.

You looked fantastic by the way,
those yellow garlands, gold ornaments,
that young moon in your hair,
impervious as gods are to every offering,
honey, curds, jaggery, thick milk.

We had a terrific time at your party.
Fabulous food. Saffron rice, roti,
moong dal, cauliflower,
dyed to marigold with turmeric.
Then, after all the celebrations,
(Tagore on the harmonium,
everyone in orange, gold and amber),
they box up all your finery
like Christmas decorations,
and throw you in a river -
your sacred clay dissolved,
to dying garlands, boluses of straw.
Awfully unfair after all you've done for folk
on pages, minds and instruments.

But there you are,
we haven't treated our gods all that well
come to think of it.

Anyway, there was me,
hoping for some inspiration,
that wisp of something left of thought,
caught on the tongue tip
before vanishing
One of your miraculous arrivals.

Sometimes I wonder if you're listening?

Note: Saraswati is the Hindu goddess of inspiration, knowledge, wisdom, arts, music and learning.

Raju says…

We judder past advertisements and signs.
'Real Touch Beauty Parlour,
Instant death. Don't touch the wire.
200 rupee fine.'

Raju stops to negotiate a skinny cow.
'Holy cow is not responsible for your vehicle.'

Raju says,
'What you write?'

'I'm a poet,' I tell him.

Raju looks blank,
he doesn't understand.

'Poetry,' I say,
groping for inspiration,
'like Tagore'.

He bows in reverence and grins.

The language of the horn
'Go slow. Accident Porn Area'

I'm a have a nice day horn a shift out of my way horn an up your arse and goad horn a cow goat on the road horn a charging straight ahead horn a better late than dead horn a wing and parping prayer horn a didn't see you there horn a ye gods that was close horn a getting up my nose horn a missed you by an inch horn a grit your teeth and flinch horn a why the bleep do that horn a don't be such a prat horn I'm behind you overtaking stopping turning left or braking tooting pooping and harassing on whichever side I'm passing no guessing gauging knowing whether here or there I'm going if I'm speeding up or slowing honking hooting blaring blowing down the broken streets you'll clatter to the sound track of Kolkata.

Grand Hotel, Kolkata

Our tea is brought,
in china thin as fingernails.
Fragrant Darjeeling,
with fruitcake jewelled with cherries,
cucumber sandwiches, thin-sliced,
triangular.

Orbs of lamplight fruit
from ornamental poles,
illuminate the baize of courtyard lawns,
the pristine tablecloths,
glint on the silver plated cutlery,
the turquoise pool
where night time bathers bask and loll
like river fish.

And here we are sipping delicious tea,
moneyed, elegant and insular,
talking of NGOs, the rural poor,
how to cure the ills of India.

Beyond a cool and pillared entrance hall,
Sikh doormen in their skirted robes, tall
ceilings with colonial cornices,
the wheezing of a punkawallah's rope
is scarcely audible.

Letter from the Raj (extract 1)

Dearest Mama, you wouldn't like it here.
It's scarcely March and yet the heat is stifling.
Jelly won't set, flour spoils, meat putrefies,
the ants, particularly troublesome.
Oh for refreshing showers of English rain!
Servants are dirty, superstitious, slow,
as black as ceremonial hats with morals of an alley cat.
They have a god for absolutely everything.
One won't serve pork, another wine.
Their stupid and profane beliefs forbid!
We need a veritable tribe to serve our needs,
for none will do another's job, and none
of them speak English, or attempt to learn,
which makes instructing them impossible.
G makes me count the silver every night,
for fear these miscreants make off with it.
We came here to bring Order
to this impious continent,
but scarcely can bring order to the house!

Punkawallah

Campanologist of air.
Patient rope-tugger.
Whoosher of charpai.
Wafter of verandah.
Heat juggler. Outsider.

He is stone deaf this one,
chosen for silent trustworthy discretion.
Under the gutter's stink, heat
heaves from earth and stuccoed walls.
Sweat drips in dust
too hot for naked feet.
A rope loops round a swollen foot and toe,
snakes through a hole
to axle and pulley in the bungalow.

All within is cool and confidential.
Domestic argument. Military discussion.
The sahib sucks his pipe,
leafs through last season's Punch,
volumes of Government reports and letters.

Memsahib oversees
ayah and dhobi, dressing boy and cook,
grumbles how indolent the servants are.
Writes to her mother.

Hour upon hour, his chest caves in and out,
mimics the heavy breathing of the punka.
And none will know his name
but 'punkawallah',
an inky thumb print in his master's ledger.

Notes: punka – a fan, especially a large swinging screen like fan hung from the ceiling and operated by a servant pulling on a rope outside. Charpai – a bedstead of woven webbing or hemp, stretched on a wooden frame and on four legs.

Letter from the Raj (extract 2)

… G plays chess and talks interminably
of going home, but never is recalled,
and anyway, what would he do in London,
being a second son? Cards and whist
pass many a tedious hour. I try to paint,
write poetry, but have no gift. Monotony
consumes our days most glutinously.
There's nothing to look forward to
but dinner parties, balls, more balls.
One cannot always entertain and dance!
I miss our three dear children every day.
G says their education's a priority
if they are not to take on heathen ways.
They say they miss their ayah when they write,
but then a letter takes so long to come.
Will they remember me when I come home?

Partition 1947
(an old man remembers)

'Where are we going?'
'I don't know,' papa said,
'but this is not my country now.
I want to die in India.'

Old eyes cloud
with seventy years of history
and loss.

'I still have dreams
of growing up with friends,
Hindu and Muslim,
Remember their addresses,
every one,
our village fish tank
with three kinds of carp,
of playing Daria Bandha in the sun,
a football we begged money for
from door to door,
the house dad built
for his retirement, back then.

The day they said
my friends were enemies,
spoke of marauding mobs,
in nearby villages.

The day
we packed up all that we could carry,
took a train.'

Flight (The Himalayas 1959)

'We must go now. We must go now,
we must go now,' my father said.
'The iron bird flies, their horses come on wheels!'

And from the savage tenor of the times,
I learn how frost can gobble noses,
blizzards bite, snow blind, and mountains fall,

how men will stalk us with their guns,
across the frozen halls of dark,
our tears and cries too loud for secrecy,

how small and sudden is goodbye,
how hope and terror weigh the same,
how many ways there are to die.

How when the moon is bright we'll hide,
or hand in hand stumble down broken stairs of night.
How tombs of snow will follow us,

men fall like boulders down ravines,
shoes shred, cold burn and friends betray.
How when one dies we will not stop or grieve.

How I will see my dad piss arcs of blood,
a crimson poppy blossoming in snow.
How still he'll carry me like faith

through air as thin as prayer and skin,
past roaring cataracts, down slithering rock,
careful as sacred culture on his back.

How when we cross to safety in this land,
I'll find a tiny patch of flowers like stars,
nuzzled in a barren cleft of stone.

How I will offer dad my sad bouquet,
and place it gently in his ruined hands.
And he will hug me in glad arms, and weep.

Refuge (Darjeeling 2016)

Balls in their colour coded wool store,
glow like sun-struck apples in a loft.
Madder root, walnut husk and indigo.

Bent fingers with long memories,
tease wool and card industriously.
Feet that have climbed through ice and sky,
tread makeshift spinning wheels.
No one looks up, they have their work to do.

Others, perhaps their daughters, crouch on stools,
bend to the clatter clunk of looms,
the bang of mallets, patter of young feet.
Phoenix and dragon climb the warp,
with cranes, mandalas,
snow-lions, lotus-flowers.

Out of the blue, one asks how old I am.
Taken aback, I tell her, show off,
pirouette on one leg like a dancer.
Lacking a common language, play the fool.
Then she says through an interpreter,
'Old women walk like this in our culture,'
crooks her back, hobbles across the floor,
mimes toothlessness to gales of laughter.

Note: following the failed Tibetan uprising against Chinese religious suppression in 1959, the Dalai Lama fled across The Himalayas to find political asylum in India. Many thousands of Tibetan refugees followed him into permanent exile. In October of that year some of them set up The Tibetan Refugee Centre, a self-supporting rehabilitation centre in the Darjeeling Himalayan hill region. The production of Tibetan handicraft, especially carpets, is the Centre's main activity.

The Scottish Cemetery, Kolkata

At first none of us would go there.
The kids were frightened of the snakes,
the tortured idols of their God.
My little boy Mohammed said he'd seen a ghost,
horned like a demon in a tree.
But when they'd cleared the jungle
dug up roots and thorns,
mended their graves
and set the stones upright,
it was like a garden in a picture book,
it smelled of mint and herbs,
whole families buried there in temples
fit for kings. Carvings of pious men,
pillars and crosses everywhere,
statues with wings, and in the summer,
birds and butterflies.
One landed on Mohammed's hand
and opened like a miracle.

We swelter in our bamboo hut
with scarcely room to swing a rat.
No shelter when it rains.
We dry our clothes and cook along the track.
Our kids play football on the rails
and dodge the trains.
So it is somewhere we can get away from that,
lower our veils when there's no man to see.
Chat over chai and biscuits while our kids run free,

learn to dance, draw, wash their hands,
write poetry, befriend the Christian ghosts
of Scots who made their homes in India,
breathe sunshine
from their greening lung of history.

Note: The Scottish Cemetery was founded as a burial ground for Presbyterians and other non Anglican denominations of Scots arriving in Calcutta in the early nineteenth century. It had fallen into disrepair but now the Scottish Cemetery Project is clearing and restoring the site and providing programmes of activities for Muslim women and children from the neighbourhood to make a tangible improvement to their lives.

Departure

Who is that woman, clothes washed for her,
clothes that were never ironed flatter,
purse tight to every needy beggar,
eyes front, keeps walking? Have I met her?

She looks like someone I knew before
I came – same height, that same demeanour,
someone who thought she had the measure
of herself, a kindlier other.

But surely that wasn't her I saw,
poking round temple, prayer and puja,
paying a pittance for a rickshaw,
bartering for discounts with the poor,

or snapping scenes of 'local colour',
kids shelling peas in roads and gutters,
a legless man dragging his kurta –
their still lifes caught behind a shutter?

Who boards that air-cooled 'plane, I wonder?
Had she been her kind familiar,
could she ever have been something more
than memsahib with her punkawallah?

Dancing girl

Dogs, cows, palms, hills, grass,
bronzed with dust to statuary,
then splashed with yellow,
orange, purple, sapphire, green.
A brown girl dressed in coloured silk
for dancing in.

Indigo Dreams Publishing
24 Forest Houses
Halwill
Beaworthy
Devon
EX21 5UU
www.indigodreams.co.uk